Temples of India

Temples of India

Krishna Deva

Vol. II: Plates

Aryan Books International
New Delhi

TEMPLES OF INDIA

ISBN: 978-81-7305-053-4 (Vol. II)
978-81-7305-054-1 (Set)

First Published: 1995
Third Reprint: 2015

Published by:
Aryan Books International
Pooja Apartments, 4B, Ansari Road, New Delhi-110 002 (India)
Tel.: 23287589, 23255799; Fax: 91-11-23270385
E-mail: aryanbooks@gmail.com
www.aryanbooks.co.in

Designed and Printed in India by
ABI Prints & Publishing Co., New Delhi

List of Plates

I

1. Sanchi. Shrines (circular and rectangular) gifted to the Buddha at Jetavana. c. 1st century B.C.
2. Sanchi. Naga Shrine with ridged octagonal dome and a leaf-thatched hut. c. 1st century B.C.
3. Barabar. Entrance to Lomash Rishi Cave. 3rd century B.C.
4. Mathura. Model of a three-storeyed octagonal shrine. c. A.D. 2nd century

II

5. Sanchi. Temple 17. c. A.D. 400
6. Tigawa. Kankali-Devi Temple. c. A.D. 400-425
7. Nachna. Parvati Temple. c. A.D. 475
8. Nachna. Parvati Temple, doorway
9. Nachna. Parvati Temple, doorway detail
10. Bhumara. Siva Temple, back view. c. A.D. 475-500
11. Bhumara. Siva Temple, Mahishasuramardini
12. Bhitargaon. Brick Temple. c. A.D. 425-450.
13. Bhitargaon. Brick Temple, *sikhara*
14. Deori (Madhia). Vamana Temple. c. A.D. 475-500
15. Deogadh. Gupta Temple. c. A.D. 500
16. Deogadh. Gupta Temple, platform detail
17. Deogadh. Gupta Temple, doorway
18. Deogadh. Gupta Temple, Nara-Narayana panel
19. Darra. Gupta Temple. c. A.D. 400-425
20. Darra. Gupta Temple, *sukanasa*
21. Udaigiri. Cave 5, Mahavaraha. c. A.D. 402
22. Pawaya. Terraced Vishnu Temple. c. A.D. 425
23. Rajgir. Maniyar Math, stucco figures. c. A.D. 575-600
24. Nalanda. Site 3, Fifth period Temple. c. A.D. 575-600
25. Bodhgaya. Mahabodhi Temple. c. A.D. 600-625
26. Nalanda. Stone Temple 2. c. A.D. 650

27. Nalanda. Stone Temple 2, *Vidyadhara*
28. Ramgadh. Mundesvari Temple. A.D. 636
28A. Aphsad. Brick Temple, niche depicting Ramayana episode at Chitrakuta. c. A.D. 675

III

29. Tala. Jethani Temple of Rudra-Bhairava. c. A.D. 575-600
30. Tala. Jethani Temple of Rudra Bhairava, front view
31. Tala. Jethani Temple of Rudra Bhairava, door-jamb detail
32. Rajim. Rajivalochana Temple. c. A.D. 600
33. Rajim. Rajivalochana Temple, carvings on door-jamb
34. Rajim. Rajivalochana Temple, doorway detail
35. Sirpur. Lakshmana Temple. c. A.D. 625-650
36. Sirpur. Lakshmana Temple, south face detail (courtesy: Michael Meister)
37. Sirpur. Lakshmana Temple, *ghanadvara* on south *bhadra*
38. Sirpur. Lakshmana Temple, doorway detail
39. Palari. Siddhesvara Temple. c. A.D. 650-675
40. Palari. Siddhesvara Temple, south *jangha* detail (courtesy: Michael Meister)
41. Palari. Siddhesvara Temple, Yamuna on door jamb
42. Dhobini. Siva Temple. c. A.D. 700-725

IV

43. Gop. Old Siva Temple. c. A.D. 550
44. Gop. Old Siva Temple, front view
45. Gop. Old Siva Temple, Uma in a *sikhara* niche
46. Bileswar. Bilvanath Temple. c. A.D. 600-625
47. Bhanasara. Temple, No.2. c. A.D. 625-650
48. Sutrapada. Surya Temple. c. A.D. 675-700
49. Akhodar. Surya Temple. c. A.D. 675-700
50. Roda. Temple No.3. c. A.D. 775-800
51. Roda. Temple No.4. c. A.D. 800
52. Ghumli. Ganesa Shrine. c. A.D. 900
53. Wadhawan. Ranakdevi Temple. c. A.D. 900
54. Kotai (Kutch). Siva Temple. c. A.D. 950
55. Kotai (Kutch). Sun Temple. c. A.D. 950

V

56. Chhapara. Mandapika Shrine. c. A.D. 600
57. Mahua. Mandapika Shrine of Siva. c. A.D. 650-675
58. Mahua. Siva Temple (No.2). c. A.D. 675
59. Kuchdon. Kuraiya Bir Temple. c. A.D. 750
60. Naresar. Group of Temples. c. A.D. 725-750

61. Naresar. Durga Temple. c. A.D. 725-750
62. Amrol. Ramesvara Mahadeva Temple. c. A.D. 725-750
63. Gwalior. Teli-ka-mandir. c. A.D. 750
64. Gwalior. Teli-ka-mandir, *vedibandha*
65. Gwalior. Teli-ka-mandir, west *jangha*
66. Gwalior. Teli-ka-mandir, Yamuna on doorway
67. Indor. Siva Temple. c. A.D. 775
68. Batesara. Siva Temple (No.3). c. A.D. 750-775

VI

69. Bhuvaneshwar. Parasuramesvara Temple. c. A.D. 650
70. Bhuvaneshwar. Parasuramesvara Temple, figures in *jala-vatayana*
71. Rameswara. Durga Shrine, early 8th century A.D.
72. Bhuvaneshwar. Vaital Deul, c. A.D. 750
73. Bhuvaneshwar. Vaital Deul, west *jangha*
74. Bhuvaneshwar. Vaital Deul, *nayika* on west *jangha*
75. Bhuvaneshwar. Vaital Deul, ornate *ghatapallava* on *vedibandha*
76. Bhuvaneshwar. Sisiresvara Temple. c. A.D. 750
77. Baramba. Simhanatha Temple. c. A.D. 800-825
78. Baramba. Simhanatha Temple, south face of *mandapa*
79. Baramba. Somanatha Temple. c. A.D. 800-825
80. Baramba. Somanatha Temple, doorway
81. Mukhalingam. Madhukesvara Temple complex. c. A.D. 800-825
82. Mukhalingam. Madhukesvara Temple, *sikhara*
83. Mukhalingam. Madhukesvara Temple, Saiva legends on south doorway of architrave *mandapa*
84. Mukhalingam. Madhukesvara Temple, *salabhanjika* on south doorway of *mandapa*
85. Mukhalingam. Madhukesvara Temple, mithuna on south doorway of *mandapa*
86. Mukhalingam. Madhukesvara Temple complex, SW corner shrine
87. Mukhalingam. Madhukesvara Temple complex, SW corner shrine
88. Mukhalingam. Somesvara Temple, ornate niche on east *jangha*. c. A.D. 850-875
89. Bodogram. Narasimhanatha Temple. c. A.D. 850

VII

90. Aihole. Huchchimalli Temple. c. A.D. 700
91. Aihole. Tarappa Temple. c. A.D. 715-730
92. Aihole. Huchchapayya Temple. c. A.D. 730
93. Pattadkal. Galagnatha Temple. c. A.D. 685-696
94. Pattadkal. Jambulinga Temple. c. A.D. 696-720
95. Pattadkal. Papanatha Temple. c. A.D. 720-740

VIII

96. Alampur. Kumara-Brahma Temple, porch pillar detail. c. A.D. 640
97. Alampur Svarga-Brahma Temple. c. A.D. 681-696
98. Alampur. Svarga-Brahma Temple, *mandapa*, south wall
99. Alampur. Garuda-Brahma Temple, *sikhara*. c. A.D. 696-733
100. Alampur. Garuda-Brahma Temple, *mandapa*, south wall
101. Alampur. Garuda-Brahma Temple, *mandapa*, south wall, carvings on *vedibandha* moulding
102. Alampur. Visva-Brahma Temple. c. A.D. 696-733
103. Alampur. Visva-Brahma Temple, south wall niches

IX

104. Deogadh. Temple No.15. c. A.D. 775
105. Deogadh. Temple No.15. seated Jina
106. Deogadh. Temple No.12. c. A.D. 775
107. Deogadh. Temple No.12. south *jangha*
108. Deogadh. Temple No.12. *sukanasa*
109. Terahi. Siva Temple. c. A.D. 800-825
110. Terahi. Siva Temple, south *jangha* detail
111. Badoh. Gadarmal Temple. c. A.D. 850
112. Badoh. Gadarmal Temple, south face
113. Badoh. Gadarmal Temple, *mandapa*
114. Badoh. Gadarmal Temple, doorway detail
115. Umri. Sun Temple. c. A.D. 850
116. Umri. Sun Temple, south face
117. Madkheda. Sun Temple. c. A.D. 850-875
118. Madhkeda. Sun Temple, front view showing *sukanasa*
119. Gwalior. Chaturbhuja Temple. A.D. 875
120. Gyaraspur. Maladevi Temple, sanctum *sikhara*. c. A.D. 850-875
121. Gyaraspur. Maladevi Temple, *vedibandha*
122. Gyaraspur. Maladevi Temple, *mandapa* detail
123. Gyaraspur. Maladevi Temple, Jaina Yakshi on *jangha*
124. Gyaraspur. Maladevi Temple, porch
125. Gyaraspur. Maladevi Temple, Jina figures above ambulatory doorway
126. Barwasagar. Jarai Math. c. A.D. 900
127. Barwasagar. Jarai Math, *jangha* detail
128. Barwasagar. Jarai Math, doorway
129. Barwasagar. Jarai Math, doorway architraves

X

130. Abaneri. Harshat Mata Temple. c. A.D. 800
131. Abaneri. Harshat Mata Temple, loving *mithuna*

132. Osian. Siva Temple No.1. c. A.D. 700
133. Osian. Harihara Temple No.1. c.725-750
134. Osian. Harihara Temple No.2. c. A.D. 750-775
135. Osian. Harihara Temple No.2, *sikhara* detail
136. Osian. Harihara Temple No.2. doorway
137. Osian. Sun Temple No.2. c. A.D. 750-775
138. Osian. Pipla Devi Temple. c. A.D. 800-825
139. Osian. Pipla Devi Temple, *vedibandha* and *jangha*
140. Osian. Mahavira Temple. c. A.D. 750-775
141. Osian. Mahavira Temple, *mandapa* roof
142. Osian. Shrines in Mahavira Temple compound. c. 10th-11th century A.D.
143. Chittor. Kalikamata Temple. c. A.D. 700
144. Chittor. Kalikamata Temple, *mandapa* interior
145. Chittor. Kalikamata Temple, dwarf pillars of *mandapa* balcony
146. Chittor. Kumbhashyama Temple. c. A.D. 700-750
147. Chittor. Kumbhashyama Temple, south balcony of sanctum
148. Buchkala. Siva Temple. A.D. 815
149. Auwa. Kamesvara Temple. c. A.D. 800-825
150. Bhawanipur. Naktimata Temple. c. A.D. 850-875
151. Baroli. Group of Temples. c. A.D. 10th century
152. Baroli. Ghatesvara Temple. A.D. 925 (*rangamandapa* added in 975)
153. Baroli. Ghatesvara Temple, Nataraja in *bhadra* niche
154. Baroli. Ghatesvara Temple, *mandapa*
155. Baroli. Ghatesvara Temple, *Apsara* on *mandapa* pillar
156. Kekind. Nilakanthesvara Temple, *rangamandapa*. c. A.D. 950
157. Jagat. Ambikamata Temple. c. A.D. 960
158. Jagat. Ambikamata Temple, sculptural decor on west *jangha*
159. Jagat. Ambikamata Temple, sculptural decor on north *jangha*
160. Jagat. Ambikamata Temple, *mandapa* ceiling
161. Nagda. Sas Bahu Temple Complex, Sas Temple. c. A.D. 975
162. Nagda. Sas Temple, sculptural decor on *mandapa* transept
163. Nagda. Sas Temple, *mandapa* interior
164. Kiradu. Small Siva Temple. c. A.D. 1050
165. Kiradu. Siva Shrine No.3, *kati*, c. A.D. 1075

XI

166. Khajuraho Group of Temples. c. A.D. 10th century
167. Khajuraho. Brahma Temple. c. A.D. 9th century
168. Khajuraho. Lakshmana Temple. c. A.D. 950
169. Khajuraho. Lakshmana Temple, *surasundari* playing with ball
170. Khajuraho. Lakshmana Temple, *surasundari* writing letter

171. Khajuraho. Lakshmana Temple, *surasundari* looking into mirror
172. Khajuraho. Lakshmana Temple, Putana-vadha
173. Khajuraho. Lakshmana Temple, Balarama killing Suta Lomaharshana
174. Khajuraho. Lakshmana Temple, hunting scene on platform
175. Khajuraho. Lakshmana Temple, *mandapa* ceiling
176. Khajuraho. Parsvanatha Temple. c. A.D. 950-970
177. Khajuraho. Parsvanatha Temple, *surasundari* applying paint
178. Khajuraho. Parsvanatha Temple, sculptures on south *jangha*
179. Khajuraho. Ghantai Temple. 10th century A.D.
180. Khajuraho. Visvanatha Temple. A.D. 1002
181. Khajuraho. Visvanatha Temple, *Apsara* playing flute
182. Khajuraho. Jagadambi Temple, south *jangha*. c. A.D. 1000-1025
183. Khajuraho. Jagadambi Temple, amorous *mithuna*
184. Khajuraho. Kandariya Mahadeva Temple. c. A.D. 1025-1035
185. Khajuraho. Kandariya Mahadeva Temple, *sikhara*
186. Khajuraho. Kandariya Mahadeva Temple, sculptures on *jangha*
187. Khajuraho. Kandariya Mahadeva Temple, *Apsara* plucking thorn
188. Khajuraho. Javari Temple. c. A.D. 1075-1100
189. Khajuraho. Adinatha Temple. c. A.D. 1075-1100
190. Khajuraho. Duladeo Temple. c. A.D. 1100-1150

XII

191. Bandhogadh. Temple, No.2. c. A.D. 775-800
192. Nachna. Chaturmukha Mahadeva Temple. c. A.D. 850
193. Nachna. Chaturmukha Mahadeva Temple, *sikhara*
194. Nachna. Chaturmukha Mahadeva Temple, *kati*
195. Nachna. Chaturmukha Mahadeva Temple, *Chaturmukha Sivalinga*
196. Nachna. Chaturmukha Mahadeva Temple, Gupta period window
197. Chandrehe. Siva Temple. c. A.D. 950
198. Chandrehe. Siva Temple, *kati*
199. Nohta. Siva Temple. c. A.D. 950-960
200. Nohta. Siva Temple, sculptures on south *jangha*
201. Bheraghat. Chausath Yogini Temple. c. A.D. 10th century
202. Bheraghat. Chausath Yogini Temple, Yogini figure
203. Maihar. Gala Math. c. A.D. 975
204. Singhpur Arjula. Panchmath, doorway. c. A.D. 10th century

XIII

205. Surwaya. Sarvatobhadra shrine on *matha* roof. c. A.D. 925
206. Kadwaha. Vaishnava Temple, No.1. c. A.D. 950-1000
207. Kadwaha. Temple No.3. c. A.D. 950-1000

208. Kadwaha. Siva Temple No.4. c. A.D. 950-1000
209. Kadwaha. Siva Temple No.5. c. A.D. 950-1000
210. Terahi. *torana*. c. A.D. 950-975
211. Terahi. Mohajmata Temple. c. A.D. 950-975
212. Gyaraspur. Athkhambha (Siva Temple). A.D. 982
213. Gyaraspur. Hindola Torana. c. A.D. 950-975
214. Suhania. Kakanmadh Temple. A.D. 1015-1035
215. Suhania, Kakanmadh Temple, Ganesa
216. Suhania. Kakanmadh Temple, Varuna
217. Suhania. Kakanmadh Temple, Devi
218. Gwalior. Larger Sas Bahu Temple. A.D. 1093
219. Gwalior. Larger Sas Bahu Temple, *mandapa* interior
220. Gwalior. Smaller Sas Bahu Temple
221. Gwalior. Smaller Sas Bahu Temple, *pitha* and *vedibandha*
222. Gwalior. Smaller Sas Bahu Temple, detail of *mandapa* ceiling

XIV

223. Udaypur. Udayesvara Temple. c. A.D. 1070-1080
224. Udaypur. Udayesvara Temple, *pitha* and *vedibandha*
225. Udaypur. Udayesvara Temple, *jangha*
226. Udaypur. Udayesvara Temple, *varandika* and *sikhara* base
227. Udaypur. Udayesvara Temple, *sikhara* top
228. Udaypur. Udayesvara Temple, figures of *sukanasa*
229. Jamli, Jamalesvara Temple. c. A.D. 1080-1100.
230. Un.Nilakanthesvara Temple. c. A.D. 1075-1100
231. Nemawar. Siddhesvara Temple. c. A.D. 1150
232. Nemawar. Siddhesvara Temple, decor on wall
233. Alirajapur. Malavai Temple. c. 14th century A.D.
234. Ambarnath. Ambarnath Temple. A.D. 1060
235. Jhodga. Mankesvara Temple. c. A.D. 1150
236. Sinnar. Gondesvara Temple. c. A.D. 1200-1225
237. Menal. Mahanalesvara Temple. c. A.D. 1100
238. Ramgadh. Bhand Deora. c. A.D. 1125
239. Bijolian. Undesvara Temple. c. A.D. 1150
240. Jhalrapatan. Sun Temple. c. A.D. 1125
241. Chittorgadh. Adbhutnath Temple. c. 16th century A.D.

XV

242. Kumbhariya. Mahavira Temple, *trika-mandapa*. A.D. 1062
243. Abu. Vimala Vasahi, *sabha mandapa* ceiling. A.D. 1031
244. Abu. Luna Vasahi, interior details of pillars and *toranas*. A.D. 1230

245. Abu. Luna Vasahi, interior of *sabha-mandapa*. A.D. 1230
246. Abu. Luna Vasahi, *sabha mandapa* ceiling. A.D. 1230
247. Ranakpur. Dharana Vihara (Adinatha Temple). A.D. 1439-1459

XVI

248. Modhera. Sun Temple, *sabha mandapa*. A.D. 1026
249. Delmal. Limbojimata Temple, wall decor. c. A.D. 1050-1075
250. Sejakpur. Navlakha Temple, south. c. A.D. 1125
251. Sejakpur. Navlakha Temple, *mandapa* transept
252. Khandosan. Hinglajmata Temple, west. A.D. 1150
253. Ghumli. Navlakha Temple, south. c. A.D. 1200
254. Ghumli. Navlakha Temple, wall decor
255. Girnar Group of Jaina Temples. c. 12th-16th centuries
256. Taranga. Ajitanatha Temple, southwest. A.D. 1165

XVII

257. Bhuvaneshwar. Muktesvara Temple, northeast. c. 10th century
258. Bhuvaneshwar. Rajarani Temple, southwest. c. 11th century
259. Bhuvaneshwar. Rajarani Temple, *pitha* and *vedibandha*
260. Bhuvaneshwar. Rajarani Temple, south *jangha*
261. Bhuvaneshwar. Lingaraja Temple, northeast. c. 11th century
262. Bhuvaneshwar. Ananta Vasudeva Temple. A.D. 1278
263. Konarka. Sun Temple, *jagamohana*. 13th century A.D.
264. Konarka. Sun Temple, drummer on *jagamohana* roof

XVIII

265. Brahmaur. Lakshana Devi Temple, pillared *mandapa*. c. A.D. 700
266. Brahmaur. Lakshana Devi Temple, pillar detail
267. Brahmaur. Lakshana Devi Temple, doorway *uttaranga* with a later (9th century) crowning gable
268. Brahmaur. Lakshana Devi Temple, bronze image of Lakshana Devi
269. Chhatrarhi. Sakti Temple, *mandapa* ceiling. c. A.D. 710
270. Chhatrarhi. Sakti Temple, entrance doorway, detail
271. Chhatrarhi. Sakti Temple, pillar detail
272. Chhatrarhi. Sakti Temple, sanctum doorway, *uttaranga*
273. Chhatrarhi. Sakti Temple, bronze image of Sakti
274. Palethi. Sun Temple. c. A.D. 675-700
275. Palethi. Sun Temple, doorway detail
276. Jageshwar. Group of Temples. c. 8th to 12th centuries
277. Jageshwar. Lakulisa Temple, southwest. c. A.D. 725-750
278. Jageshwar. Nataraja Temple, west. c. A.D. 725-750

279. Jageshwar, Navadurga Temple. c. A.D. 775
280. Jageshwar. Chandrika Temple. c. A.D. 825
281. Lakhamandal. Siva Temple. c. A.D. 750
282. Lakhamandal. loose *sukanasa* fragment
283. Jagatsukh. Siva Temple. c. A.D. 800-825
284. Bajaura. Basheshar Mahadeva Temple. c. A.D. 850
285. Bajaura. Basheshar Mahadeva Temple, Ganga on doorway
286. Bajaura. Basheshar Mahadeva Temple, Mahishasura-mardini in north *bhadra*
287. Masrur. Main Siva Temple, wall decor. c. A.D. 800-825
288. Masrur. Ornate niche frame of a minor shrine
289. Masrur. Varuna seated on *makara*
290. Chamba. Group of Temples dedicated to Siva and Vishnu. c. 10th to 16th centuries
291. Baijnath. Siva Temple, general view. c. early 13th century
292. Baijnath. Siva Temple, detail of main sanctum

XIX

293. Mattan. Martanda Temple, northeast. c. A.D. 725-750
294. Avantipur. Avantisvami Temple, peristyle and two subsidiary shrines. c. A.D. 850-860
295. Avantipur. Avantisvami Temple, part view of peristyle
296. Avantipur. Avantisvami Temple, stair panel showing Kamadeva with two consorts
297. Avantipur. Avantisvami Temple, stair panel depicting Avantivarman worshipping
298. Buniar. Vishnu Temple, northwest. c. A.D. 900-926
299. Buniar. Vishnu Temple, peristyle, northeast corner
300. Pandrethan. Siva Temple, south. c. 10th century A.D.
301. Pandrethan. Siva Temple, carvings on ceiling
302. Payar. Siva Temple, north c. A.D. 950-975

XX

303. Mahabalipuram. Pancha-Pandava Rathas. c. A.D. 630-668
304. Mahabalipuram. Arjuna Ratha
304A. Mahabalipuram. Nakula-Sahadeva Ratha
305. Mahabalipuram. Shore Temple. A.D. 700-728
306. Kalugumalai. Vettuvankovil. c. A.D. 800
307. Narttamalai. Vijayalaya-Cholisvara. c. A.D. 850
308. Kodumbalur. Muvarkovil. c. A.D. 880
309. Kodumbalur. Muvarkovil, Kalari Siva
310. Thanjavur. Brihadisvara Temple. c. A.D. 1000-1018
311. Gangaikondacholapuram. Brihadisvara Temple. c. A.D. 1035
312. Gangaikondacholapuram. Brihadisvara Temple, Chandesanugrahamurti
313. Darasuram. Airavatesvara Temple. c. A.D. 1146-1173
314. Darasuram. Airavatesvara Temple, *Mandapa* interior

315. Darasuram. Airavatesvara Temple, *Rishi-patnis* tempted by Bhikshatana Siva
316. Tribhuvanam. Kampaharesvara Temple. c. A.D. 1187-1218
317. Kumbhakonam. Nagesvarasvami Complex. Nataraja Temple, chariot-shaped *mandapa*. c. 13th century A.D.
318. Vijayanagara. Vitthala Temple, *mahamandapa*. A.D. 1516
319. Vijayanagara. Vitthala Temple, stone *ratha*
320. Vijayanagara. Pampapati Temple, east *gopura*. A.D. 1510
321. Vijayanagara. Hazara Rama Temple, Amman shrine. A.D. 1521
322. Vellore. Jalakanthesvara Temple, *kalyanamandapa* (Horse-court). c. A.D. 1625-1650
323. Madurai. Minakshi Temple, south *gopura*. c. A.D. 1625-1650
324. Somanathpur. Kesava Temple. A.D. 1268
325. Somanathpur. Kesava Temple, *adhishthana* friezes
326. Belur. Chennakesava Temple, *madanika*. A.D. 1117

Plates

1. Sanchi. Shrines (circular and rectangular) gifted to the Buddha at Jetavana. c. 1st century B.C.

2. Sanchi. Naga Shrine with ridged octagonal dome and a leaf-thatched hut. c. 1st century B.C.

3. Barabar. Entrance to Lomash Rishi Cave. 3rd century B.C.

4. Mathura. Model of a three-storeyed octagonal shrine. c. A.D. 2nd century

5. Sanchi. Temple 17. c. A.D. 400

6. Tigawa. Kankali-Devi Temple. c. A.D. 400-425

7. Nachna. Parvati Temple. c. A.D. 475

8. Nachna. Parvati Temple, doorway

9. Nachna. Parvati Temple, doorway detail

10. Bhumara. Siva Temple, back view. c. A.D. 475-500

11. Bhumara. Siva Temple, Mahishasuramardini

12. Bhitargaon. Brick Temple. c. A.D. 425-450.

13. Bhitargaon. Brick Temple, *sikhara*

14. Deori (Madhia). Vamana Temple. c. A.D. 475-500

15. Deogadh. Gupta Temple. c. A.D. 500

16. Deogadh. Gupta Temple, platform detail

17. Deogadh. Gupta Temple, doorway

18. Deogadh. Gupta Temple, Nara-Narayana panel

19. Darra. Gupta Temple. c. A.D. 400-425

20. Darra. Gupta Temple, *sukanasa*

21. Udaigiri. Cave 5, Mahavaraha. c. A.D. 402

22. Pawaya. Terraced Vishnu Temple. c. A.D. 425

23. Rajgir. Maniyar Math, stucco figures. c. A.D. 575-600

24. Nalanda. Site 3, Fifth period Temple. c. A.D. 575-600

25. Bodhgaya. Mahabodhi Temple. c. A.D. 600-625

26. Nalanda. Stone Temple 2. c. A.D. 650

27. Nalanda. Stone Temple 2, *Vidyadhara*

28. Ramgadh. Mundesvari Temple. A.D. 636

28A. Aphsad. Brick Temple, niche depicting Ramayana episode at Chitrakuta. c. A.D. 675

29. Tala. Jethani Temple of Rudra-Bhairava. c. A.D. 575-600

30. Tala. Jethani Temple of Rudra Bhairava, front view

31. Tala. Jethani Temple of Rudra Bhairava, door-jamb detail

32. Rajim. Rajivalochana Temple. c. A.D. 600

33. Rajim. Rajivalochana Temple, carvings on door-jamb

34. Rajim. Rajivalochana Temple, doorway detail

35. Sirpur. Lakshmana Temple. c. A.D. 625-650

36. Sirpur. Lakshmana Temple, south face detail (courtesy: Michael Meister)

37. Sirpur. Lakshmana Temple, *ghanadvara* on south *bhadra*

38. Sirpur. Lakshmana Temple, doorway detail

39. Palari. Siddhesvara Temple. c. A.D. 650-675

40. Palari. Siddhesvara Temple, south *jangha* detail (courtesy: Michael Meister)

41. Palari. Siddhesvara Temple, Yamuna on door jamb

42. Dhobini. Siva Temple. c. A.D. 700-725

43. Gop. Old Siva Temple. c. A.D. 550

44. Gop. Old Siva Temple, front view

45. Gop. Old Siva Temple, Uma in a *sikhara* niche

46. Bileswar. Bilvanath Temple. c. A.D. 600-625

47. Bhanasara. Temple, No.2. c. A.D. 625-650

48. Sutrapada. Surya Temple. c. A.D. 675-700

49. Akhodar. Surya Temple. c. A.D. 675-700

50. Roda. Temple No.3. c. A.D. 775-800

51. Roda. Temple No.4. c. A.D. 800

52. Ghumli. Ganesa Shrine. c. A.D. 900

53. Wadhawan. Ranakdevi Temple. c. A.D. 900

54. Kotai (Kutch). Siva Temple. c. A.D. 950

55. Kotai (Kutch). Sun Temple. c. A.D. 950

56. Chhapara. Mandapika Shrine. c. A.D. 600

57. Mahua. Mandapika Shrine of Siva. c. A.D. 650-675

58. Mahua. Siva Temple (No.2). c. A.D. 675

59. Kuchdon. Kuraiya Bir Temple. c. A.D. 750

60. Naresar. Group of Temples. c. A.D. 725-750

61. Naresar. Durga Temple. c. A.D. 725-750

62. Amrol. Ramesvara Mahadeva Temple. c. A.D. 725-750

63. Gwalior. Teli-ka-mandir. c. A.D. 750

64. Gwalior. Teli-ka-mandir, *vedibandha*

65. Gwalior. Teli-ka-mandir, west *jangha*

66. Gwalior. Teli-ka-mandir, Yamuna on doorway

67. Indor. Siva Temple. c. A.D. 775

68. Batesara. Siva Temple (No.3). c. A.D. 750-775

69. Bhuvaneshwar. Parasuramesvara Temple. c. A.D. 650

70. Bhuvaneshwar. Parasuramesvara Temple, figures in *jala-vatayana*

71. Rameswara. Durga Shrine, early 8th century A.D.

72. Bhuvaneshwar. Vaital Deul, c. A.D. 750

73. Bhuvaneshwar. Vaital Deul, west *jangha*

74. Bhuvaneshwar. Vaital Deul, *nayika* on west *jangha*

75. Bhuvaneshwar. Vaital Deul, ornate *ghatapallava* on *vedibandha*

76. Bhuvaneshwar. Sisiresvara Temple. c. A.D. 750

77. Baramba. Simhanatha Temple. c. A.D. 800-825

78. Baramba. Simhanatha Temple, south face of *mandapa*

79. Baramba. Somanatha Temple. c. A.D. 800-825

80. Baramba. Somanatha Temple, doorway

81. Mukhalingam. Madhukesvara Temple complex. c. A.D. 800-825

82. Mukhalingam. Madhukesvara Temple, *sikhara*

83. Mukhalingam. Madhukesvara Temple, Saiva legends on south doorway of architrave *mandapa*

84. Mukhalingam. Madhukesvara Temple, *salabhanjika* on south doorway of *mandapa*

85. Mukhalingam. Madhukesvara Temple, mithuna on south doorway of *mandapa*

86. Mukhalingam. Madhukesvara Temple complex, SW corner shrine

87. Mukhalingam. Madhukesvara Temple complex, SW corner shrine

88. Mukhalingam. Somesvara Temple, ornate niche on east *jangha*. c. A.D. 850-875

89. Bodogram. Narasimhanatha Temple. c. A.D. 850

90. Aihole. Huchchimalli Temple. c. A.D. 700

91. Aihole. Tarappa Temple. c. A.D. 715-730

92. Aihole. Huchchapayya Temple. c. A.D. 730

93. Pattadkal. Galagnatha Temple. c. A.D. 685-696

94. Pattadkal. Jambulinga Temple. c. A.D. 696-720

95. Pattadkal. Papanatha Temple. c. A.D. 720-740

96. Alampur. Kumara-Brahma Temple, porch pillar detail. c. A.D. 640

97. Alampur Svarga-Brahma Temple. c. A.D. 681-696

98. Alampur. Svarga Brahma Temple, *mandapa*, south wall

99. Alampur. Garuda-Brahma Temple, *sikhara*. c. A.D. 696-733

100. Alampur. Garuda-Brahma Temple, *mandapa*, south wall

101. Alampur. Garuda-Brahma Temple, *mandapa*, south wall, carvings on *vedibandha* moulding

102. Alampur. Visva-Brahma Temple. c. A.D. 696-733

103. Alampur. Visva-Brahma Temple, south wall niches

104. Deogadh. Temple No.15. c. A.D. 775

105. Deogadh. Temple No.15. seated Jina

106. Deogadh. Temple No.12. c. A.D. 775

107. Deogadh. Temple No.12. south *jangha*

108. Deogadh. Temple No.12. *sukanasa*

109. Terahi. Siva Temple. c. A.D. 800-825

110. Terahi. Siva Temple, south *jangha* detail

111. Badoh. Gadarmal Temple. c. A.D. 850

112. Badoh. Gadarmal Temple, south face

113. Badoh. Gadarmal Temple, *mandapa*

114. Badoh. Gadarmal Temple, doorway detail

115. Umri. Sun Temple. c. A.D. 850

116. Umri. Sun Temple, south face

117. Madkheda. Sun Temple. c. A.D. 850-875

118. Madhkeda. Sun Temple, front view showing *sukanasa*

119. Gwalior. Chaturbhuja Temple. A.D. 875

120. Gyaraspur. Maladevi Temple, sanctum *sikhara*. c. A.D. 850-875

121. Gyaraspur. Maladevi Temple, *vedibandha*

122. Gyaraspur. Maladevi Temple, *mandapa* detail

123. Gyaraspur. Maladevi Temple, Jaina Yakshi on *jangha*

124. Gyaraspur. Maladevi Temple, porch

125. Gyaraspur. Maladevi Temple, Jina figures above ambulatory doorway

126. Barwasagar. Jarai Math. c. A.D. 900

127. Barwasagar. Jarai Math, *jangha* detail

128. Barwasagar. Jarai Math, doorway

129. Barwasagar. Jarai Math, doorway architraves

130. Abaneri. Harshat Mata Temple. c. A.D. 800

131. Abaneri. Harshat Mata Temple, loving *mithuna*

132. Osian. Siva Temple No.1. c. A.D. 700

133. Osian. Harihara Temple No.1. c.725-750

134. Osian. Harihara Temple No.2. c. A.D. 750-775

135. Osian. Harihara Temple No.2, *sikhara* detail

136. Osian. Harihara Temple No.2. doorway

137. Osian. Sun Temple No.2. c. A.D. 750-775

138. Osian. Pipla Devi Temple. c. A.D. 800-825

139. Osian. Pipla Devi Temple, *vedibandha* and *jangha*

140. Osian. Mahavira Temple. c. A.D. 750-775

141. Osian. Mahavira Temple, *mandapa* roof

142. Osian. Shrines in Mahavira Temple compound. c. 10th-11th century A.D.

143. Chittor. Kalikamata Temple. c. A.D. 700

144. Chittor. Kalikamata Temple, *mandapa* interior

145. Chittor. Kalikamata Temple, dwarf pillars of *mandapa* balcony

146. Chittor. Kumbhashyama Temple. c. A.D. 700-750

147. Chittor. Kumbhashyama Temple, south balcony of sanctum

148. Buchkala. Siva Temple. A.D. 815

149. Auwa. Kamesvara Temple. c. A.D. 800-825

150. Bhawanipur. Naktimata Temple. c. A.D. 850-875

151. Baroli. Group of Temples. c. A.D. 10th century

152. Baroli. Ghatesvara Temple. A.D. 925 (*rangamandapa* added in 975)

153. Baroli. Ghatesvara Temple, Nataraja in *bhadra* niche

154. Baroli. Ghatesvara Temple, *mandapa*

155. Baroli. Ghatesvara Temple, *Apsara* on *mandapa* pillar

156. Kekind. Nilakanthesvara Temple, *rangamandapa*.
c. A.D. 950

157. Jagat. Ambikamata Temple. c. A.D. 960

158. Jagat. Ambikamata Temple, sculptural decor on west *jangha*

159. Jagat. Ambikamata Temple, sculptural decor on north *jangha*

160. Jagat. Ambikamata Temple, *mandapa* ceiling

161. Nagda. Sas Bahu Temple Complex, Sas Temple. c. A.D. 975

162. Nagda. Sas Temple, sculptural decor on *mandapa* transept

163. Nagda. Sas Temple, *mandapa* interior

164. Kiradu. Small Siva Temple. c. A.D. 1050

165. Kiradu. Siva Shrine No.3, *kati*, c. A.D. 1075

166. Khajuraho Group of Temples. c. A.D. 10th century

167. Khajuraho. Brahma Temple. c. A.D. 9th century

168. Khajuraho. Lakshmana Temple. c. A.D. 950

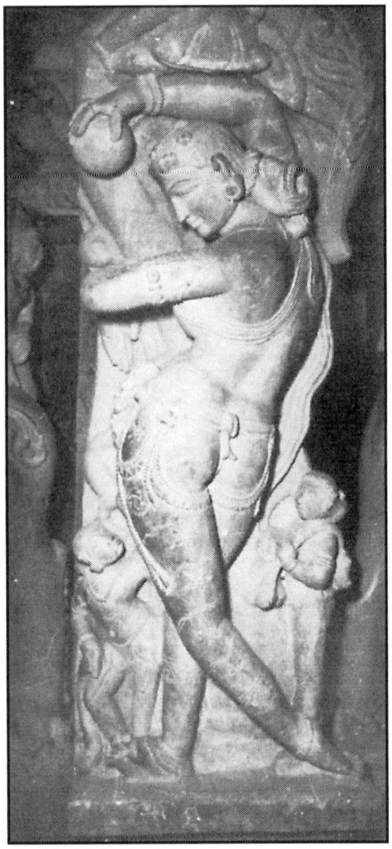

169. Khajuraho. Lakshmana Temple, *surasundari* playing with ball

170. Khajuraho. Lakshmana Temple, *surasundari* writing letter

171. Khajuraho. Lakshmana Temple, *surasundari* looking into mirror

172. Khajuraho. Lakshmana Temple, Putana-vadha

173. Khajuraho. Lakshmana Temple, Balarama killing Suta Lomaharshana

174. Khajuraho. Lakshmana Temple, hunting scene on platform

175. Khajuraho. Lakshmana Temple, *mandapa* ceiling

176. Khajuraho. Parsvanatha Temple. c. A.D. 950-970

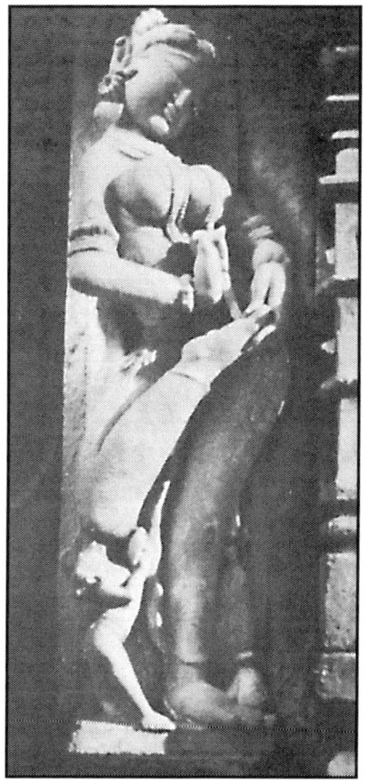

177. Khajuraho. Parsvanatha Temple, *surasundari* applying paint

178. Khajuraho. Parsvanatha Temple, sculptures on south *jangha*

179. Khajuraho. Ghantai Temple. 10th century A.D.

180. Khajuraho. Visvanatha Temple. A.D. 1002

181. Khajuraho. Visvanatha Temple, *Apsara* playing flute

182. Khajuraho. Jagadambi Temple, south *jangha*. c. A.D. 1000-1025

183. Khajuraho. Jagadambi Temple, amorous *mithuna*

184. Khajuraho. Kandariya Mahadeva Temple. c. A.D. 1025-1035

185. Khajuraho. Kandariya Mahadeva Temple, *sikhara*

186. Khajuraho. Kandariya Mahadeva Temple, sculptures on *jangha*

187. Khajuraho. Kandariya Mahadeva Temple, *Apsara* plucking thorn

188. Khajuraho. Javari Temple. c. A.D. 1075-1100

189. Khajuraho. Adinatha Temple. c. A.D. 1075-1100

190. Khajuraho. Duladeo Temple. c. A.D. 1100-1150

191. Bandhogadh. Temple, No.2. c. A.D. 775-800

192. Nachna. Chaturmukha Mahadeva Temple. c. A.D. 850

193. Nachna. Chaturmukha Mahadeva Temple, *sikhara*

194. Nachna. Chaturmukha Mahadeva Temple, *kati*

195. Nachna. Chaturmukha Mahadeva Temple, *Chaturmukha Sivalinga*

196. Nachna. Chaturmukha Mahadeva Temple, Gupta period window

197. Chandrehe. Siva Temple. c. A.D. 950

198. Chandrehe. Siva Temple, *kati*

199. Nohta. Siva Temple. c. A.D. 950 960

200. Nohta. Siva Temple, sculptures on south *jangha*

201. Bheraghat. Chausath Yogini Temple. c. A.D. 10th century

202. Bheraghat. Chausath Yogini Temple, Yogini figure

203. Maihar. Gala Math. c. A.D. 975

204. Singhpur Arjula. Panchmath, doorway. c. A.D. 10th century

205. Surwaya. Sarvatobhadra shrine on *matha* roof. c. A.D. 925

206. Kadwaha. Vaishnava Temple, No.1. c. A.D. 950-1000

207. Kadwaha. Temple No.3. c. A.D. 950-1000

208. Kadwaha. Siva Temple No.4. c. A.D. 950-1000

209. Kadwaha. Siva Temple No.5. c. A.D. 950-1000

210. Terahi. *torana*. c. A.D. 950-975

211. Terahi. Mohajmata Temple. c. A.D. 950-975

212. Gyaraspur. Athkhambha (Siva Temple). A.D. 982

213. Gyaraspur. Hindola Torana. c. A.D. 950-975

214. Suhania. Kakanmadh Temple. A.D. 1015-1035

215. Suhania, Kakanmadh Temple, Ganesa

216. Suhania. Kakanmadh Temple, Varuna

217. Suhania. Kakanmadh Temple, Devi

218. Gwalior. Larger Sas Bahu Temple. A.D. 1093

219. Gwalior. Larger Sas Bahu Temple, *mandapa* interior

220. Gwalior. Smaller Sas Bahu Temple

221. Gwalior. Smaller Sas Bahu Temple, *pitha* and *vedibandha*

222. Gwalior. Smaller Sas Bahu Temple, detail of *mandapa* ceiling

223. Udaypur. Udayesvara Temple. c. A.D. 1070-1080

224. Udaypur. Udayesvara Temple, *pitha* and *vedibandha*

225. Udaypur. Udayesvara Temple, *jangha*

226. Udaypur. Udayesvara Temple, *varandika* and *sikhara* base

227. Udaypur. Udayesvara Temple, *sikhara* top

228. Udaypur. Udayesvara Temple, figures of *sukanasa*

229. Jamli, Jamalesvara Temple. c. A.D. 1080-1100.

230. Un.Nilakanthesvara Temple. c. A.D. 1075-1100

231. Nemawar. Siddhesvara Temple. c. A.D. 1150

232. Nemawar. Siddhesvara Temple, decor on wall

233. Alirajapur. Malavai Temple. c. 14th century A.D.

234. Ambarnath. Ambarnath Temple. A.D. 1060

235. Jhodga. Mankesvara Temple. c. A.D. 1150

236. Sinnar. Gondesvara Temple. c. A.D. 1200-1225

237. Menal. Mahanalesvara Temple. c. A.D. 1100

238. Ramgadh. Bhand Deora. c. A.D. 1125

239. Bijolian. Undesvara Temple. c. A.D. 1150

240. Jhalrapatan. Sun Temple. c. A.D. 1125

241. Chittorgadh. Adbhutnath Temple. c. 16th century A.D.

242. Kumbhariya. Mahavira Temple, *trika-mandapa*. A.D. 1062

243. Abu. Vimala Vasahi, *sabha mandapa* ceiling. A.D. 1031

244. Abu. Luna Vasahi, interior details of pillars and *toranas*. A.D. 1230

245. Abu. Luna Vasahi, interior of *sabha-mandapa*. A.D. 1230

246. Abu. Luna Vasahi, *sabha mandapa* ceiling. A.D. 1230

247. Ranakpur. Dharana Vihara (Adinatha Temple). A.D. 1439-1459

248. Modhera. Sun Temple, *sabha mandapa*. A.D. 1026

249. Delmal. Limbojimata Temple, wall decor. c. A.D. 1050-1075

250 Sejakpur. Navlakha Temple, south. c. A.D. 1125

251. Sejakpur. Navlakha Temple, *mandapa* transept

252. Khandosan. Hinglajmata Temple, west. A.D. 1150

253. Ghumli. Navlakha Temple, south. c. A.D. 1200

254. Ghumli. Navlakha Temple, wall decor

255. Girnar Group of Jaina Temples. c. 12th-16th centuries

256. Taranga. Ajitanatha Temple, southwest. A.D. 1165

257. Bhuvaneshwar. Muktesvara Temple, northeast. c. 10th century

258. Bhuvaneshwar. Rajarani Temple, southwest. c. 11th century

259. Bhuvaneshwar. Rajarani Temple, *pitha* and *vedibandha*

260. Bhuvaneshwar. Rajarani Temple, south *jangha*

261. Bhuvaneshwar. Lingaraja Temple, northeast. c. 11th century

262. Bhuvaneshwar. Ananta Vasudeva Temple. A.D. 1278

263. Konarka. Sun Temple, *jagamohana*. 13th century A.D.

264. Konarka. Sun Temple, drummer on *jagamohana* roof

265. Brahmaur. Lakshana Devi Temple, pillared *mandapa*. c. A.D. 700

266. Brahmaur. Lakshana Devi Temple, pillar detail

267. Brahmaur. Lakshana Devi Temple, doorway *uttaranga* with a later (9th century) crowning gable

268. Brahmaur. Lakshana Devi Temple, bronze image of Lakshana Devi

269. Chhatrarhi. Sakti Temple, *mandapa* ceiling. c. A.D . 710

270. Chhatrarhi. Sakti Temple, entrance doorway, detail

271. Chhatrarhi. Sakti Temple, pillar detail

272. Chhatrarhi. Sakti Temple, sanctum doorway, *uttaranga*

273. Chhatrarhi. Sakti Temple, bronze image of Sakti

274. Palethi. Sun Temple. c. A.D. 675-700

275. Palethi. Sun Temple, doorway detail

276. Jageshwar. Group of Temples. c. 8th to 12th centuries

277. Jageshwar. Lakulisa Temple, southwest. c. A.D. 725-750

278. Jageshwar. Nataraja Temple, west. c. A.D. 725-750

279. Jageshwar, Navadurga Temple. c. A.D. 775

280. Jageshwar. Chandrika Temple. c. A.D. 825

281. Lakhamandal. Siva Temple. c. A.D. 750

282. Lakhamandal. loose *sukanasa* fragment

283. Jagatsukh. Siva Temple.
c. A.D. 800-825

284. Bajaura. Basheshar Mahadeva Temple.
c. A.D. 850

285. Bajaura. Basheshar Mahadeva Temple, Ganga on doorway

286. Bajaura. Basheshar Mahadeva Temple, Mahishasura-mardini in north *bhadra*

287. Masrur. Main Siva Temple, wall decor. c. A.D. 800-825

288. Masrur. Ornate niche frame of a minor shrine

289. Masrur. Varuna seated on *makara*

290. Chamba. Group of Temples dedicated to Siva and Vishnu. c. 10th to 16th centuries

291. Baijnath. Siva Temple, general view. c. early 13th century

292. Baijnath. Siva Temple, detail of main sanctum

293. Mattan. Martanda Temple, northeast. c. A.D. 725-750

294. Avantipur. Avantisvami Temple, peristyle and two subsidiary shrines. c. A.D. 850-860

295. Avantipur. Avantisvami Temple, part view of peristyle

296. Avantipur. Avantisvami Temple, stair panel showing Kamadeva with two consorts

297. Avantipur. Avantisvami Temple, stair panel depicting Avantivarman worshipping

298. Buniar. Vishnu Temple, northwest. c. A.D. 900-926

299. Buniar. Vishnu Temple, peristyle, northeast corner

300. Pandrethan. Siva Temple, south. c. 10th century A.D.

301. Pandrethan. Siva Temple, carvings on ceiling

302. Payar. Siva Temple, north c. A.D. 950-975

303. Mahabalipuram. Pancha-Pandava Rathas. c. A.D. 630-668

304. Mahabalipuram. Arjuna Ratha

304A. Mahabalipuram. Nakula-Sahadeva Ratha

305. Mahabalipuram. Shore Temple. A.D. 700-728

306. Kalugumalai. Vettuvankovil. c. A.D. 800

307. Narttamalai. Vijayalaya-Cholisvara. c. A.D. 850

308. Kodumbalur. Muvarkovil. c. A.D. 880

309. Kodumbalur. Muvarkovil, Kalari Siva

310. Thanjavur. Brihadisvara Temple. c. A.D. 1000-1018

311. Gangaikondacholapuram. Brihadisvara Temple. c. A.D. 1035

312. Gangaikondacholapuram.
Brihadisvara Temple,
Chandesanugrahamurti

313. Darasuram. Airavatesvara Temple.
c. A.D. 1146-1173

314. Darasuram. Airavatesvara Temple, *Mandapa* interior

315. Darasuram. Airavatesvara Temple, *Rishi-patnis* tempted by Bhikshatana Siva

316. Tribhuvanam. Kampaharesvara Temple. c. A.D. 1187-1218

317. Kumbhakonam. Nagesvarasvami Complex. Nataraja Temple, chariot-shaped *mandapa*. c. 13th century A.D.

318. Vijayanagara. Vitthala Temple, *mahamandapa*. A.D. 1516

319. Vijayanagara. Vitthala Temple, stone *ratha*

320. Vijayanagara. Pampapati Temple, east *gopura*. A.D. 1510

321. Vijayanagara. Hazara Rama Temple, Amman shrine. A.D. 1521

322. Vellore. Jalakanthesvara Temple, *kalyanamandapa* (Horse-court). c. A.D. 1625-1650

323. Madurai. Minakshi Temple, south *gopura*. c. A.D. 1625-1650

324. Somanathpur. Kesava Temple. A.D. 1268

325. Somanathpur. Kesava Temple, *adhishthana* friezes

326. Belur. Chennakesava Temple, *madanika*. A.D. 1117